Youps

Ruth Richman

First Published in 2025 by Blossom Spring Publishing
Youps Copyright © 2025 Ruth Richman
ISBN 978-1-917938-28-0
E: admin@blossomspringpublishing.com
W: www.blossomspringpublishing.com
Ruth Richman as the author and Jen Edwards as the illustrator,
have been asserted in accordance with the Copyright, Designs and Patents Act,1988.

My heartfelt thanks to my lifelong friend,
Jen Edwards, who made this book come alive with
her wonderful illustrations, and to the staff and pupils at
Forest School in Timperley for their feedback.

Youps is a light-hearted tale written mostly in rhyming couplets, about an abandoned dog in France. I have imagined what happened until he reached the rescue centre, but the story of his adoption is true.

Youps was his name at the animal home, and this little dog became a much-loved part of our family and our life, sharing the excitement whilst we were living in France.

We had emigrated from the UK to live just outside a small French village and stayed there quite happily until our first grandchild came along. The family ties were too strong to ignore, so we returned to be part of the lives of our grandchildren, of which there are three to date.

This book had its beginnings in a restaurant, in an effort to occupy a little one after she'd finished her meal. The story made its way slowly into written words then quickly popped up as the rhyme you see now.

There is so much more to tell you about Youps, that I wonder if there's another rhyme waiting to be written.

Extras: Having taught at primary schools, I have included a quiz at the end of the book to help children get the most from the story.
There is also a link to Youps' Instagram account, where you can see some actual photographs of him.

P.S. As his name is French, it is said like this, 'You-ps.'

This book is for all children, everywhere,
but especially for Evie, Hugo and Louis,
who all love dogs.

Youps

This is a story, lots of it true
And I've written it, my darlings, just for you.
It happened not here, but over in France,
And you must go there, if you ever have chance.

We loved our five years living mid countryside
Travelling far, sometimes travelling wide.
The people were lovely right from the start
But this pup was my best friend, stealing my heart.

Contents

1. Unwanted

Once upon a time, this was a real, live time,
Before this pup was even going to be mine,
He lived with some people who were not too kind
But Pup, being Pup, didn't really seem to mind.

He ran down their hallway, around every room
Chewing their shoes and the end of a broom.
His best fun of all was to jump on a bed,
But this was quite naughty, or so they had said.

They'd not taken time to train him, you see,
Nor cuddled or talked to him, whilst on their knee.
They did not quite know that pups needed so much
Like discipline and walks and loving and such.

There was a small yard at the back of the house -
No room to run, not least for a mouse.
With washing and toys and mud underfoot,
It wasn't a nice place for our little mutt.

He'd grown in size but had still not grown up
And carried on acting just like a pup.
This pup wasn't wanted, nor was he loved.
He sometimes got knocked and he often got shoved.

They shouted and scolded him day upon day,
Which just made Pup think that he might run away.
His food wasn't fresh, and his water was stale,
The adults ignored him, the kids pulled his tail.

As time went on by, they all grew quite cross
And wondered if anyone might feel his loss.
So, the dad took him out one day in his van,
Then left him alone – what a terrible man!

First Pup was excited (for he never went out)
'Til he saw the van going, then was in no doubt
That he had to find shelter, he had to find food,
He had to find people who weren't quite so rude.

2. Lost

The pup started walking, he did not know where,
To find some new people to love him and care.
He longed for a home with some outdoor space,
Dreamed as he walked with a smile on his face.

Then rain fell quite heavily around and about;
It soaked through his fur, in his ears, up his snout.
So he shook off the drops with a shake and a twist
Then saw a large gate through the rain and the mist.

The pup needed sleep, it was getting quite late,
So he peered through the bars on the firmly closed gate.
He had to make sure there was no one else there
So he might close his eyes with never a care.

Slipped under the gate without so much as a sound
Standing quite still, looking quickly around.
He saw a large oak tree not too far away
With grass underneath that seemed like some hay.

It was long, it was dry and crunched under his feet
'A great bed to lie on. Oh, what a treat!'
The pup was asleep before you could say, "Stay!"
And he slept until sunrise, the start of next day.

The bird songs and cockerels were such a delight
He forgot all his troubles, he forgot his own plight.
He sniffed at the grass and sniffed in the air
Trying to decide to go which way, or where.

Breakfast was first on his list of to-dos
But then he heard hooves and a lot of cows' moos.
So up jumped the pup, but his exit was blocked,
Cows circling around him, seeming quite shocked.

Towards our small pup, one cow bent her head.
She stopped all her chewing and then gently said,
'You look rather dirty and wet through and through.
Whatever has happened to poor little you?'

The story unfolded from beginning to now,
With nothing but horror on the face of each cow.
'I'm hungry and thirsty and need to find food.
Please don't detain me. I'm not in the mood.'

The cows had a conflab and talked it all through
One just looking on with a slow, lazy chew.
The cow bent again and looked into Pup's eyes
'We don't know a lot, but try this for size …

Squeeze through that thorn hedge, so wide and so dark
And carry on going 'til you find the park.
It's people who go there, take children to play
And eat picnic lunches, but throw some away.

You might find a morsel of stuff left behind.
Whatever it is, you won't have to mind.
We wish you good luck as you pass us on by.'
Then the cow shook her head and gave a loud sigh.

Pup smiled a big, 'Thanks,' then ran through their feet
Wondering what he'd now find, to drink or to eat.
With eyes tightly shut and minding his nose
Through the dark hedge he went on the tips of his toes.

The park wasn't far, and no one was there,
Unless you count Brereton, the carved wooden bear!

Pup did a quick air-sniff, smelled what was around
Then ran to a table and searched on the ground.

He jumped on the table, found a stale crust,
Crisps that were soggy, but eat them he must.
Saw half a sausage all covered in mud
But ate it regardless, and boy, was it good!

Down from the table and in only one bound
Reached an old waste bin. Now, what had he found?
Pup tugged at the corner with all of his might
And made a small hole – what a great sight!

Out dropped some rubbish which he pawed to one side
Pulled again at the hole to make it quite wide.
He sniffed out a pot all covered in goo
Which he licked until clean. That tasted good too!

He heard a faint squeaking, behind him, he thought,
So he turned but saw nothing, no one, nought.
Then, a pile of fresh earth began to appear
And out popped a mole, with no trace of fear.

'I heard the cows talking and wanted to see
If I may be of help, just between you and me?'
Mole set down a worm from the earth he'd just dug,
Which started to burrow 'til mole gave it a tug!

'I mostly eat earthworms, the odd spider and snail,'
Mole said to the pup, who suddenly turned pale.
'I'm happy to share whatever I find
I try to be thoughtful, friendly and kind.'

'Your kindness is welcome, but I am quite full,
And my diet can only be said to be dull.
For I don't like food that's soft and goes 'squish'
Like grubs and worms, they're not my sort of dish.'

He thanked the mole kindly for showing his care
Then all of a sudden, the mole wasn't there!
Finding an apple, which he crunched to the core,
Pup left the bin open, not looking for more.

He lay on the grass, licking paw left and right –
He must get cleaned up; he looked such a sight.
Then, Pup soon decided to make his next move
To carry on walking - he'd much left to prove.

3. Found

Having had a good scratch, then stretching his back,
Pup left the small park by following a track.
He trundled and padded alongside the road
When a car passed him by, then gradually slowed.

A man called out, "Here, little dog, here."
Then stepped out of his car as the pup drew near.
He held out a hand for the pup to come sniff,
Which he did unafraid, he was there in a jiff.

The man stroked the pup as he searched for a collar,
But finding one missing, felt sad for the fella.
Feeling sorry to see what a state Pup was in
He wanted to help him, but where to begin?

"I would take you home now, but I live in a flat,
No garden - I know you dogs don't like that."
Placing the pup on the seat of his car,
The man simply explained that they wouldn't go far.

Just to a dogs' home, they'd be really quick
And he hoped that this pup was never car-sick!
After a while, the car came to a stop,
Through trees, in a car park, on a hill, near the top.

The man walked away, Pup up on his seat,
Stared through the window, seeing whom he might meet.

A girl came to greet him, her smile showing hope
As she nipped back inside to fetch a short rope.

Opening the door so the Pup could jump down
The man looked quite sad, and he started to frown.
The girl said, "We thank you for bringing him here.
We'll find him new people who'll think he's a dear."

She slipped the rope around his neck as they stood
And watched as the man drove off through the wood.
Where was he now, and what would happen next?
He felt a bit lonely and a little perplexed.

He stood there, not moving, looked up at the girl
Who smiled at him kindly, turned round with a twirl.
She knew in her heart that he'd be a good pet
There'd be lots to do, and he wasn't there yet.

They passed a small sign at the side of the road
And said, "Hi," to a driver, delivering his load.
Pup tucked in beside her, avoiding her step
Then his mood quickly lifted - he felt full of pep!

To walk anywhere on a rope was so grand,
Not be in a yard where he just had to stand.
But he'd had enough walking with no end in sight
As he'd wished for some comfort, a bed for the night.

The girl made him feel he was safe and secure.
At this moment in time, he couldn't ask for more.
He'd go with the flow and see what transpired
But boy oh boy, did he suddenly feel tired.

(La SPA – Société Protectrice des Animaux.)

4. Rescued

"Come along with me, my little lost friend.
We'll make you smile, your needs we will tend.
A bed and a blanket, some food and fresh water,
All dogs should have these; they all really ought to."

Pup followed the girl to an old dusty barn
And listened intently as she told him a yarn
Of others passing through, not ages before,
But sadly, she thought there were bound to be more.

She led the young pup to a pen all his own,
His bowls and his bed he was then shown.
"I'll leave you alone to find your way round,
Then pop back to fetch you. Now, don't make a sound."

He sniffed at the blanket inside the bed,
Smelled another dog-surely, this was their bed instead!
He looked all around him, his nose in the air,
Couldn't find the other dog, one just wasn't there.

So, he trampled the blanket, lay down with a sigh,
Closed his eyes, dreaming 'til lunchtime was nigh.

His stomach was churning, 'Please let me eat.
Don't care what it is, doesn't have to be meat.'

The din that awoke him from dreams of good times
Startled him awake, no alarm or clock chimes.
He lifted his head to look here and there
To see what made noises that gave him a scare.

A boy passed by whistling as he went on his round,
To fill every bowl and to feed every hound.
The lad spoke so nicely to each one and all,
The tall and the short ones, the big and the small.

"I'll give you some extra, I can see that you're new,
Can't have you go hungry - afraid it's not stew!
This stuff is called kibble, dogs like it, I'm told,
It's hard and it's crunchy and tasty and cold."

As soon as the bowl was put down on the floor,
The pup scoffed the lot and wished there was more.
Back came the girl with a short rope in hand
To take him across a bit of wasteland.

They walked to a building, to a room oh so bright
Which smelled of new things that gave him a fright.
This place was a vet's clinic - clean, fresh and calm
Where he met a nice lady, full of dog charm.

Up, on a table, the vet looked at his teeth,
Felt up his back and then underneath.
She stuck a thermometer up his rear end
Which was not a nice thing, he wouldn't pretend!

The vet then picked up a syringe and a needle
And gripped by his scruff, Pup started to wheedle.
A sharp stinging feeling Pup felt in his neck
Made him dive from the table and onto the deck.

The pup couldn't wait to get out of the door
Pulling the rope, his neck a bit sore.
"You're fine little dog, so please don't you fret
The vet says you're healthy, which makes a good pet."

Towards a new pen he was led on his lead
Past so many dogs, too many indeed.
His pen he could see he was going to share
With a wire-haired terrier, who was already there.

The girl led Pup in saying, "This is Tibou
Now I must pick a name that I think best suits you.
You all have to have a brand new name
For no dogs' at this dog's home can be called the same."

Closing the pen, she walked over the yard
To the office, meantime, thinking quite hard.
They had a good way of naming each dog
In lists that they held in an alphabet log.

A	Anais	N	Nana
B	Bertrande	O	Odette
C	Channel	P	Pascal
D	Delphine	Q	Quincy
E	Enzo	R	Rene
F	Franc	S	Souris
G	Gaston	T	Tibou
H	Henri	U	Ulysse
I	Isabel	V	Vivienne
J	Jupe	W	Walter
K	Kooky	X	Xavier
L	Lyon	Y	
M	Mojette	Z	

(I'm explaining this story, but only in part,
Why Youps and Tibou sounded odd at the start.
This tale all took place in an overseas land.
These names are all French, now you'll understand.)

Names starting with A had got up to the X
So the girl had to find one with Y, which was next.
"Youps," she said brightly, please make a note,
She asked the receptionist, who then quickly wrote ...

Youps

Pup became Youps for his time at this home,
And alongside Tibou both wished they could roam
Through fields, along lanes as dogs love to do,
Sniffing the hedgerows and other dogs' poo!

They stayed in their pen for most of their days,
Each other for company, in beds they would laze.
Sleeping and eating and pacing the wire -
This was no life, in fact, it was dire!

Tibou wasn't handsome, in fact quite a mess,
With all over curls (he looked odd, I confess)
And Youps looked bedraggled, his fur was too long.
They'd bathed him last week, so he now didn't pong!

If they were lucky, and people walked by,
They'd run around their pen to catch their eye.
Luckier still they'd be taken for a run,
The two dogs together, never taking just one.

A playground was there for fun and for games,
Where they knew other dogs, but never their names.
With tyres to jump over and logs to run round,
The noise of their barking, an ear-splitting sound.

High jumps and tunnels to go over and through
(I'd like to go there. What about you?)
The dogs had such fun each time they came out,
Running and chasing each other about.

With playtime soon over, it was on with their leads
For a walk down the lane, which every dog needs.
The lane led to a field of hedges and grass
With a pond in the middle, which they then had to pass.

Never were dogs let off their long lead,
As some might run off and take no heed
Of the calls and the shouting to please come on back,
As most enjoy freedom to run with the pack.

Then back to their pen, more tired and quite glad
To think of the fun and the good time they'd had.
Once more, the routine came round every day -
Sleeping and pacing with no walks or play.

The dogs who had been at the centre a while
Could teach a newcomer to sit and to smile.
So Tibou told young Youps a load of new stuff
To help him with people, as they could be tough.

The most important things about people are:

1. Going for walks

Don't pull people when you are on your lead. They are supposed to be
taking you for a walk, not the other way around!

2. Playing with other dogs

Always ask another dog if it wants to play. If you are too bouncy, some dogs will pretend to nip you to tell you to cool it!

3. Keeping clean

You will have a bath from time to time so try and enjoy it. You will feel better afterwards. You'll also get a good brushing now and again. However, there are dog brushes and there are dog brushes! Some have very spikey teeth which can bite you and yelping doesn't help the process.

4. Living with people- this list was endless ...

- don't jump up at them
- don't growl at them
- don't go through gates before them
- don't pee or poo in their house
- don't get their car all muddy
- don't trump when you are sitting by their feet because dog trumps really do smell awful
- chewing their slippers is a definite no-no
- if you are soaking wet, don't shake yourself too close to them ... they don't like it
- be a guard dog and bark your head off if anyone comes to the door

- lick their face to tell them that you love them
- be careful not to use your teeth when
  you take stuff from their hands
- be quiet when they say so
- look at them when they talk to you
- chase any cats or squirrels that come into
  their garden
- wag your tail when they come home and
  you may get a biscuit
- don't jump onto the sofa without being
  invited to do so
- be careful of babies and small children, as
  they fall over very easily
- be on your best behaviour when they take you out 'cos they like to show
  people how well they have trained you
- just ignore them when they pick up your poo ... goodness knows what they
  do with it!

Youps listened very quietly to all Tibou said
Then both of the dogs took themselves off to bed.
He wished that he'd known some of this as a pup
Then maybe he wouldn't have had such hard luck.

His days he spent listening to sounds round about
Heard bird song and talking, and just the odd shout.
Heard cars stopping, starting, doors slamming shut,
Then, 'Oi! Get off Youps - you're sat on my foot!

5. The Search

Now not long before this all took place
A couple left England to live at slow pace.
In the middle of France, found their own bit of heaven
Down a lane with houses just numbering seven.

With fields all around them, a château next door,
The peace and the quiet - who could want more?
Their village was small and ever so quaint
With many a shutter done in blue paint.

Waking in quiet countryside every morn,
Hear cockerels crowing as new days are born.
It's a life they'd just dreamed of, how lucky were they
To move to this country, not too far away?

They'd bought an old house made entirely of stone
In a very large garden, they really couldn't moan.
Plenty of room to run and to play
When family and friends came out there to stay.

Her name was Penny, his name was Joe.
They'd started to look many long months ago
For a dog for her birthday, that had just gone by.
The task was enormous, but still, they must try.

Penny's sister was already living close by,
Had friends with dogs, so she phoned them to try.
"I'll ask if they know of the sort you are after -
Smallish and furry," then she heard Penny's laughter!

These friends helped out at a refuge for pooches,
Raised money for food and helped with their mooches.
Had dogs of their own all adopted on sight
Felt sorry for all, seeing them in such plight.

No luck for Penny, there just wasn't her kind,
So on with her search, she really mustn't mind.
She'd find one quite soon as she knew in her heart
That her dog was there waiting, a new life to start.

She searched on the internet, dogs' homes galore,
Saw photos, read stories, and had to know more.
Joe takes out his map to see where they are
Decides some are too far to go in the car.

Dogs' stories were written with fun and some jokes
To tug at the heartstrings of all sorts of folks.
Some appeared to be written by the dogs on their own
All pleading with people to, 'Please take me home!'

Date taken in: 12-8-2017   Rescue centre: SPA Poitiers
Name: Anais   Ref: 17-247D
Rottweiler cross, black   Born around: 23-7-2015

I am not fierce, but I am just very noisy around other dogs because I want to play. I enjoy going for long walks. I do not look very handsome because I have had parts of my ears, and my tail cut off. I have never had anyone to love me and am looking for kind people and a nice, forever home.

Date taken in: 6-1-2018   Rescue centre: SPA Poitiers
Name: Mojette   Ref: 18-008D
Labrador, chocolate   Born around: 18-9-2015

I have always lived outside but could go into a room at the end of the house. I can jump 1.2m over the garden wall and enjoy running away. Also living at my house are 2 cats for me to chase and a 4-year-old boy to play with, although I am a bit rough with him. I like to chew things, and I do not like carrots.

There were rescue centres for beasts large and small
That amazed Joe and Penny, who read through them all!

Dogs,
    cats,
        horses,
            rabbits,
                pet birds,
                    squirrels,
                        wild birds,
                            hedgehogs,
                                battery hens,
                                    large farm animals,
                                        reptiles and amphibians,
                                            rodents and small mammals.

They couldn't believe it, caught both unawares
There was even a centre for unwanted bears!

They drove by an animal shelter one day,
So stopped to see dogs please, if they may.
There was one poor creature who just couldn't stand,
Was shaking with fear at the touch of a hand.

To witness the cruelty that some dogs had had
Made Penny and Joe feel incredibly sad.
Many dogs stayed there and that wasn't all,
For a barn full of cats was behind a high wall.

Their dog wasn't there amongst all they had met,
They hadn't yet found their own special pet.
So back to the internet, more searching to do
Until they could say, "We've found you! It's true!"

Some owners choose dogs that have the same hair
(or the same face, but let's not go there!)
Now Penny has a mop of unruly tresses,
Hair just as she likes it, she often confesses.

So, her hunt was for one that was not ultra sleek,
That looked a bit scruffy (like her, dare I speak?)
Being drawn to a pup with a curly, long mane
Would be like her own-they'd look just the same!

Finding two photos she greatly admired
Of dogs seeming dirty, hungry and tired,
She called out to Joe to ask, "Near or far?"
So he looked on his map, pointing, "Here they are."

The first of these dogs' homes was too far to go -
A full hour away if you didn't go slow.
So they phoned the last refuge to check he'd not sold,
"He's still here and waiting," Penny was told.

The snap that she saw of him, eyes seeming sad,
Made Penny think that she'd make him feel glad.
Finding this pup had filled her with glee.
Could he be the one? Will he like me?

Penny and Joe set off the next day
To find out if this pup was really OK.
Feeling excited, with all fingers crossed
They followed the map, trying not to get lost.

6. Waiting for their people

Pup's time dragged so slowly, it has to be said,
And the highlight each day was when they were fed.
Until this one day when Youps woke with a start.
His stomach was churning, a fluttering heart.

He didn't quite know why he felt this way.
Was he ill or still tired? He just couldn't say.
Sometime after breakfast, about half past ten,
A couple walked up and stopped at their pen.

Dogs wait all day long and then through the night
For new people to come, and what a great sight
When someone looks in and lets out a sigh -
Then you're in with a chance if they stay close by.

Youps was first to reach the front wire.
Tibou ran beside him, some six inches higher.
Looking at the people through the corner of his eye
Youps suddenly felt so terribly shy.

They peered in their pen and said something strange
Their words were all nonsense, except for their names.
The couple were English, their words were quite odd,
Then Joe winked at both dogs and gave them a nod.

(You *can* talk to dogs - use the sound of your voice
With treats in your hand, so it gives them a choice
To do what you say, then get something nice,
Or do their own thing and miss out on the prize.)

Pup didn't dare hope that these people had come
To find him and love him and take him back home.
They waited to take both dogs out for a run
And what Youps didn't know, was that love had begun

The people who worked here were terribly kind
And did what they could, new homes to find.
But his fur was uncombed as they didn't have time
To brush and to comb dogs and make them look fine.

His eyes said it all, with delight they both shone,
He'd try best behaviour until they were gone.
He barked at them loudly to let them both know
He was perfect for them and ready to go.

He hoped that his tail wagging would let them see
His excitement was clear, 'Oh please, please take me!'
He'd been there three months, since dumped all alone
To fend for himself and to find a new home.

A girl followed shortly with leads, not a rope,
And Youps looked at Penny, hope upon hope
That he'd make them love him, and let them feel
That they were his people and know it for real.

The girl brought them out, both straining to run.
It was great to be out in the breeze and the sun.
They looked all around to the left and the right,
Making sure there was nothing to give them a fright.

Then Penny led Youps alongside Tibou
To see if he walked well, liked other dogs do.
She talked to him, watching his every move.
Stroked him to show him how much she approved.

Then onto the playground to play off their lead,
To run and to jump, no telling he'd need.
They watched how he acted with more dogs around
And rated his social skills - all fairly sound.

But out in the playground Youps did a strange thing.
He nipped Penny's thumb with no hurt or no sting!
He'd decided to tell her, his own special way,
That he felt he'd be happy if they'd take him to stay.

Luckily for him that Penny understood
That pups get quite frisky but are generally good.
She smiled at Pup's happiness, so plain to see,
Then said to Joe, "He's just perfect for me!"

They told Youps to wait for just one more night,
To not give up hope, just to sit tight.
For early tomorrow they'd be there by return
So, "Please don't you fret and please don't you yearn."

7. To adopt a dog

They went to the office to ask what to pay
To adopt a dog that had been there to stay.
So, they paid for their Youps but left him right there
And hoped very much he'd not feel despair.

For they needed to buy all things that dogs need
Like two bowls, a bed, some food and a lead.
They returned to the dogs' home the very next morning,
Walked down to his pen to find him still yawning.

As soon as he saw them, Youps barked more and more -
His folk had come back, to take him for sure!
Youps looked at Tibou, both eye to eye,
Then gruffed a dog sound meaning, 'Goodbye!'

Youps was led from his pen - his home for some time,
To the very noisy office, but that was just fine.
Feeling uncertain of just what to do
He stood by Penny, just joining the queue.

Joe turned to a display board full of dog stuff
But remembered last night when they'd bought quite enough-
Said, "Youps will have toys and playthings galore.
We've already bought plenty. He doesn't need more."

Joe hadn't bought a collar, not bought it on spec'
As they weren't quite sure on the size round Pup's neck.
Then Joe twirled a stand in the corner to find
One made of leather – just the right kind.

The office was crowded with children and dogs
Waiting for papers and new owners' Pet Logs.
Youps' tail was wagging, his excitement was clear -
He was on his way out, and home time was near.

He jumped up at a small boy who nearly fell down -
Then Joe told Youps off with a bit of a frown.
"Children are precious and not all are strong.
We must always be careful and to jump up is wrong."

Youps' papers were signed, his Pet Log transferred
With jab dates and doses, they read every word.
He even had a microchip, no extra cost,
And the number was there should he ever get lost.

250269500614093

Joe thanked them all kindly, a smile on his face,
As leaving the office they picked up their pace.
They all walked to the car park; Joe opened the back
Where Youps took a leap - he just had the knack!

He settled himself there with never a sound,
Knowing for sure, he was homeward bound.
Penny was so happy, and Joe's smile so wide,
They'd found their new pup who filled them with pride.

Pup stood at the window, looked back up the road,
Wondered if other dogs may have been sold.
When suddenly seeing his pen mate Tibou
On his way to a car – now adopted too!

'I felt in my bones that you wouldn't long be there
In our rescue home, where they love you and care.
For nice as it is, there's nothing to beat
A home of your own, now that's a real treat.'

Quizzical Questions

Try the quiz below, then you can turn to page 46 to find the answers.

1. In which country did Youps live?
2. What two things did he chew?
3. Where did Youps sleep on his first night, all alone?
4. Which animals found him in the morning?
5. Which animal was also there, carved out of wood?
6. Where did Youps find something to eat?
7. What did Youps have for his breakfast?
8. Who wanted to share worms and snails with Youps?
9. Where did the man in the car take Youps?
10. Why did this man not take Youps home?
11. What did the girl fetch to take Youps to the old barn?
12. What did this girl say all dogs ought to have?
13. Who did Youps go and see in the clinic?
14. Why didn't he like this visit?
15. Who was the other dog in Youps' pen?
16. How are the names of the new dogs chosen?
17. Name two things in the dogs' playground.
18. What must a dog not do if sitting at someone's feet?
19. How does a dog let you know that they love you?
20. Who were the two people searching for a dog?

Bonus question: Can you guess the meaning of the French words at the bottom of page 15?

Wonderful Words

Can you think of words of your own that rhyme with the ones that I have given you below? If you are struggling, you could turn to these page numbers and search for one that I have used in the story.

		Page
1.	Bow (as in a ribbon)	34
2.	Say	34
3.	Part	35
4.	Den	35
5.	Fire	36
6.	Pie	36
7.	None	37
8.	Knee	37
9.	Sight	38
10.	Glue	38
11.	Hood	39
12.	Learn	39
13.	Care	40
14.	Feed	40
15.	Puff	41
16.	Sure	41
17.	Pong	42
18.	Frost	42
19.	Hound	43
20.	Feet	43

Answers to Quizzical Questions

	Page
1. France (introduction page)	
2. Shoes and the end of a broom	1
3. In the grass underneath an oak tree	5
4. Cows	6
5. Brereton, the carved wooden bear	8
6. In a park (on a table, on the grass and from a bin)	9
7. A stale crust, soggy crisps, half a muddy sausage and some goo! (What do you think it was?)	9
8. A mole	10
9. A dogs' home	13
10. He lived in a flat, which dogs don't like	13
11. A short rope	14
12. A bed, a blanket, some food and fresh water	16
13. The vet	19
14. He was given an injection, and had his temperature taken	19
15. Tibou	21
16. In alphabetical order	21
17. Tyres, a pile of logs, a tunnel, jumps and a ramp	23
18. Trump!	25
19. The dog licks your face	25
20. Joe and Penny	28

Answer to bonus question: Animal Protection Society.

Photos

If you would like to see some photos of **Youps**, ask an adult if they could show you his Instagram account.

Username: rescue.youps, or they can just scan the QR code below:

About the Author

The author Paula Stokes has written this book under the pen name of Ruth Richman.

Paula now lives in Cheshire, returning here after retiring and spending five years living in France. She and her husband are members of the little-known group 'grandparents in childcare.'

She has been a netball coach for almost 30 years, and has enjoyed being involved with many children, young people and adults at schools and in netball clubs in the Northwest. She was also a Beaver Scout Leader for some time.

Paula has recently been tempted to return to a school environment on a part-time basis to teach games and a little practical science, drawing on her experience of working in a variety of different laboratories.

She loves her garden, plays canasta and crown green bowls, and goes to a u3a French group once a week to learn far more of the language than she ever managed in France!

As this story is based on the truth, there are some photos of *Youps* on his Instagram account for you to see the real 'him' and to follow him, if you'd like to.
Username: rescue.youps.

www.blossomspringpublishing.com